Christmas Present

James A. Hrdlicka

1st WORLD
PUBLISHING

Christmas Present

James A. Hrdlicka

© James A. Hrdlicka 2007

Published by 1stWorld Publishing
1100 North 4th St. Fairfield, Iowa 52556
tel: 641-209-5000 • fax: 641-209-3001
web: www.1stworldpublishing.com

LCCN: 2007931203
HardCover ISBN: 978-1-4218-9989-3

Questions or comments about this book may be sent to: **jahrdl@yahoo.com**

Illustrations by Char Russell
Edited by Martha B. Colby

To my mother,
who gave me life and showed me love.

To my angels, Mr. and Mrs. Smith,
who reached out to me in my time of need.
They gave me love and direction.
They showed me the Magic of Christmas.

Acknowledgements

I met Debbie in 1975 and we married three years later. She has loved me and "stood by me" day after day. Debbie has always been my biggest fan; she suggested years ago that I write this book. Although it took a while, I finally decided to follow her advice. Thank you, Debbie.

Additionally, special thanks to Amy Markus, the director of the Hancock Library, and her staff. Over a period of several months, I was a regular at the library. I used the library computer to finalize the manuscript for this book. Amy and her staff were always there, with a smile, to help me.

Table of Contents

Setting the Scene

The Magic of Christmas happens each and every year. I think it starts some time after the start of school in September. It continues as we move from late summer into fall—from late fall into early winter.

As the beauty of the fall foliage peaks and then falls, the Magic becomes more apparent. The morning air chills and the sun's rays lessen; frost coats the ground. It is in this time of transition that the Magic of Christmas begins.

With the passing of Halloween and the approach of Thanksgiving, the Magic begins to take hold. Thoughts of loved ones and Christmas come alive. "When will I begin my Christmas shopping, and what will I get for him? And for her?" And before we know it, Thanksgiving is next week—then tomorrow. Thanksgiving was yesterday!

The Magic of Christmas intensifies and flourishes! Christmas shoppers scurry about. Christmas trees appear in homes, in front yards and in the stores. Christmas lights and music and decorations are everywhere!

We see the Magic in the first snowfall and in the Christmas cards that come. The Magic is in the garland, the poinsettias, the holly, the candy canes, and in the fragrant candles that glow. It's in our churches and in the Baby Jesus manger scenes. The Magic is on the faces of our children.

And for those of us that are most fortunate, the Magic is within. The Magic is in reconnecting with our priorities. The Magic is in reconnecting with our loved ones, with ourselves, and with our inner child.

Christmas Joy

I hear a calm and gentle voice,
As I speak to my child.
A loving voice, a caring voice,
It almost sounds like me!

Awaken little child, awaken sweet, sweetheart.
A wish to be my child again,
I long for all that's me.
Wake up my beautiful child,
Wake up for me to see!

Two thousand years ago,
It started from above.
Mary gave us a beautiful child,
To be all that we could be.
It's Christmastime, sweet Christmastime,
Now a child's awoken in me!

1. Christmas in July

If you're ever in the southwest corner of New Hampshire in the town of Hancock, I'm easy to find. I'm the guy that drives the red Toyota truck with the red Christmas bow. Depending upon the season, the truck bed might contain a lawn mower, a leaf blower, or several snow shovels and a roof rake. Regardless of the season, my black Lab, Kallee, will most likely be behind me on her bed in the rear cab section. She is not only my companion but, in a sense, my "business partner."

Kallee is very patient in waiting for me to complete my daily work tasks. She will stay tied to a tree in the woods or run loose while I work, depending upon my customers and the location in town. While working for the Sandbacks on School Street, Kallee will need to stay in the truck. They have two cats!

Kallee knows that she will be rewarded for her patience because on our drive home, we almost always stop at the field behind the fire station for "a walk." She loves to play ball, sniff the scents of other dogs and wildlife and run free. After completing a day's work of mowing, or shoveling, or spring/fall clean up, I certainly don't need the exercise, but I know that she does. "She's my baby!"

Last July Greta, one of Hancock's senior citizens, asked me why I kept the red bow on the grill of my truck. I simply replied, "Christmas in July, Greta!" She looked puzzled, but smiled politely at me as she continued her walk down Norway Hill into town.

Despite the cold and "summer-less" days of the Christmas season, I try to hold onto the special feelings and emotions that surround me at this time. This world would surely be a better and safer place if Christmas could continue into January, February and beyond.

Christmas is magical.

Christmas Magic

Each Christmas is different, as each is the same.
Sometimes old and sometimes new.
It comes again with passing time.
Familiar sights and sounds have new meaning now.
We gather round a table filled with love—
And empty places.

Special are the hopes that stir alive,
The children, gifts, and Santa Claus.
A fragrant candle fills the room,
As lights and glitter glisten.

Each Christmas brings a magic.
It takes us forward to what is new.
It takes us back, for just a moment,
To Christmas Past.

2. Favorite Gifts

Each year, the Magic of Christmas inspires me. As I get older, I see Christmas in a new and different light. I enjoy writing and I always find time to write a Christmas poem in time to include with the Christmas cards I mail. The themes of my poems are generated by a current event or situation in my life. Sometimes I'm inspired by the message on a bumper sticker, a conversation with a friend, a fond memory or the beauty of winter. When I wish to share my Christmas message with the community, I'll e-mail a letter to the Monadnock Ledger newspaper in Peterborough, New Hampshire. My letter appeared in the Tuesday before Christmas 2006 edition:

CHRISTMAS MAGIC

Christmas IS the most magical time of the year. Take a look at Christmas Magic; it's all around You! I spent most of last weekend buying a Christmas tree, setting it up, "lighting it," and decorating it with "my bride." This week I spent my spare time Christmas shopping online and writing Christmas and

Chanukah cards. Meanwhile, I haven't yet started up my snow blower and there's a large pile of wood in the backyard awaiting both me and my chainsaw. I'm just too busy with Christmas; and I love it!

The Magic of Christmas is all around You! The "secret ingredient" of this Magic is: "Christmas IS what each of us brings to it."

It is about the birth of a Savior, Jesus. However, it can be about giving "our best" to others or it can be about reliving memories most dear to us. It can be about the Joy of Santa and children or about feeling like a child again! It can be about sharing time with loved ones or simply about the beauty of the winter season. It can be about a renewed Hope for Peace on Earth. Or, it can be about all of this or whatever You choose to bring to it.

Christmas is Here! "It's tapping at your window—it's rattling the tea cups." It's right here! "Do your best" to let the Magic in and "Have yourself a Merry (and Magical) Christmas!"

🎄 🎄 🎄 🎄 🎄

When returning home with Kallee, our house is quiet and chilly. The heat from the woodstove has cooled since morning. As winter's days begin to lengthen, I'm happy to get home before dark. I light the stove as quickly as I can; it will soon warm the contents of our modest log home in the woods. I prepare my dinner, but I make sure that Kallee eats first. If she is at all hungry while I eat my dinner, she will bark and carry on at the sound of the slightest noise. I wash the dishes and get the day's work receipts recorded and put away before Debbie gets home from work.

Debbie is my bride of almost thirty years. She works as a therapist in Keene, New Hampshire. She loves her work with children and adolescents. Both of us taught in public school for years, and we're each very happy with our current work.

We try to live as simple a life as possible. We were never blessed with children, so we've been able to do without cell phones and the latest electronic gadgets. Our twenty-inch television and VCR have served us well; we get three to five stations, depending upon the weather. We know that having cable and a wide-screen TV would interfere with our outdoor walks with Kallee. The snowmobile trails in the woods around our house are convenient for walking through nature's beauty.

I did spend a lot of money this past Christmas on gifts, but it was a good year for me and I do enjoy celebrating Christmas. I make sure that the gifts I give are meaningful to the recipient. It has to be a gift "from me."

I have never told Debbie that she is my best friend, but she has been just that for many years. We have our disagreements from time to time, but she has always been right there for me. I don't know what I'd do without her love and support and I hope that I'll never have to find out. I wrote, framed, and gave this poem to her for Christmas. It's been on the jelly cabinet in our living room ever since.

My Favorite Gifts Will Be. . .

Happy Holy Days—Merry Christmas to You.
Will the gifts I give be gifts from Me?
Will I give you All My Best?
Will it be enough — for You?
Will You feel my presence?

My favorite gifts will Be from You.
Thoughtfulness and Commitment—from You.
Gifts from the heart—from Your Heart,
Will Lift Me through.
My favorite Gifts will Be and Be . . .

From You.

James Hrdlicka

3. Seasons Change

Summer is my favorite season. Its long days of bright sunshine bleach my blond hair almost white as it turns my skin bronze-colored. The hottest New Hampshire days bring me joy as I walk behind my lawnmower. September begins to fade my tan and October takes it from me. The leaves fall down and the trees are bare. I often say to Debbie, "It's a good thing for Thanksgiving and Christmas, because otherwise I'd feel like crawling under a rock until springtime!" Christmas lifts my spirits; it's a special season.

A Special Season

I walk through afternoon's autumn light,
Looking for summer's warmth.
Faded rays reflect off ice-glazed pond,
Casting shadows 'cross a field.
A part of me is missing, a true love's gone,
Alone and chilled, I shiver.

Long walks are no more,
Winter winds direct me home.
Woodstove and rocker now occupy my time,
I'm thankful for a fire tonight,
With inner comfort here inside.

A winter's night then beauty white,
Miracles awaiting to be seen.
Nuthatch and chickadees, one by one,
Morning flurries fill the air.
A star up high with lights below,
Romping puppy energizes in the snow.

And I Feel the Past and All,
Its Quiet Peace, Happiness and Hope.
The Wonder of Christmas is Near.
Baby Jesus soon to be Born.
It awakens me, it brings me to my feet.
I laugh, I cry—I sing, I dance.

James Hrdlicka

4. Let It Snow

One of my fondest childhood memories is that of a winter snow-storm in Queens, New York, in 1961. We lived in a second-story apartment at 193rd Street on Jamaica Avenue in Hollis. I had never seen this much snow before! The garbage trucks plowed the snow into piles along Jamaica Avenue as high as my bedroom window. I had so much fun playing "King of the Mountain" on my mountain of snow right there in front of our apartment. More than forty years later, a winter snowstorm continues to warm my heart.

We have a 500-watt spotlight across the front yard. We light it mostly on snowy winter nights to gaze into the snowfall. With the exception of the ocean crashing onto a rocky Maine coast-line, I can think of nothing more magnificent than the sight of falling snow.

Winter Wonder

Oh gentle winter snow.
You fall lightly as a mist.
I feel you, barely, on my face,
As I strain to see your beauty in the night.

I close my eyes and dream of you.
I awaken, again, with thoughts of you.
I look to see your morning art, upon the winter
wood and rock.

You are my reason for the cold.
You warm me, glisten gently.
You are winter's promise for miracles yet to come.

🌲 🌲 🌲 🌲 🌲

In early December, a Boston tire store advertised snow tires. Their radio broadcast stated that, "If we don't get at least a foot of snow, you'll get the tires for free!" This winter, so far, has yielded the least amount of snow ever recorded—less than six inches in the Boston area. As I write on the evening of Lincoln's birthday, 2007, a foot or more of snow is forecast for tomorrow night into the following day. Looks like I won't be the only one excited about the upcoming snowstorm!

February 16 note: It snowed through Valentine's Day and into the night. We got fourteen inches in Hancock with more than two feet in the mountains—"Winter Wonderland"!

James Hrdlicka

5. Thelma

Debbie, Kallee and I just arrived home after our hike along a snowmobile trail, just beyond our home. It's most fitting for me to make mention of Thelma, on this eighteenth day in February; today is the third anniversary of Thelma's passing.

▲ ▲ ▲ ▲ ▲

I met Thelma in the fall of 2003. She was ninety-seven years old. A friend of hers had seen my ad on the bulletin board at the Hancock Market. After meeting with Thelma and her family, she had hired me to help her with her evening meal preparation. Along with doing odd jobs, I like to cook.

I arrived at Thelma's weeknights at 5 p.m. to bring her a snack and ginger ale, stoke the kitchen woodstove, and warm up the noodles and tomato sauce that Thelma's friend, Ellie, had prepared that afternoon. Thelma always had a small serving of rice pudding or custard for dessert.

While Thelma ate her dinner and dessert, I'd do the dishes and we'd talk. She was curious about my daily activities. She'd thoughtfully ask me about Debbie and Kallee. She was a kind, considerate person, and grateful for my help. It was an honor to be there.

I wished that I had known Thelma in her younger years. She had told me that she would have liked to have met me sooner, too. Thelma missed her days of hiking through the woods with her family. She was full of life, but her body was not keeping up with her spirit. She now had to depend upon a walker to get from room to room. She would often say, "Getting old is not for sissies." Thelma was no sissy.

Before leaving Thelma's, I would stoke the stove according to Thelma's specifications. She asked that I use small pieces of wood to get the stove fired up, and just the right number of larger pieces to fill the stove. That small woodstove would need to keep her home warm through the night until Neal, the groundskeeper, arrived early the next morning. On occasion, the stove would burn itself out before morning light; I'd be sure to "hear about it" the next day, upon arriving.

As Christmas approached, Thelma confided in me that she hadn't yet written her annual Christmas note to her lifelong friends. She told me that she couldn't get into the spirit of Christmas because of all the turmoil in the world. Our involvement in Iraq had her particularly troubled. Thelma would jokingly say that if she didn't write her Christmas note and mail it, her friends would think that she was dead.

I tried to cheer her up, but I was unsuccessful. She was too distressed with world events to fully enjoy Christmas in her cozy country home. Friends and family visited her regularly. Thelma had almost all of what any ninety-seven-year-old woman could want. She was too preoccupied with world matters to realize this.

She had lived a complete life and she was well respected in the community. For her environmental efforts in Hancock, The Harris Center for Conservation Education had dedicated their new conference room to her.

I felt badly for Thelma. At the time, I thought that this could be her last Christmas, and she wouldn't allow herself to fully enjoy it. It was her last Christmas.

Thelma let her "Merry Christmas" get away! Few of us will ever know which Christmas will be our last. Since Thelma's passing, I am so much more aware of the importance of living each Christmas as though it could be my last.

"I couldn't sleep this early morn.
Instead I dreamed, of . . .

My Last Christmas."

Winter Beauty—Music
Family—Friends—Sweet Angels
Giving—Receiving

Let My Christmas Last!
Let Me Live It,
Let Me Feel It,
    This Time.

My Father—My Mary—My Jesus
Only They Will Know
Only They Can Know,
     Of...
My Last Christmas.

6. All about Me

I feel blessed in living a simple life. Many people that I know live in homes that are several times the size of my home. The silver and antiques in their homes are probably worth more than the value of my home! Some drive Jaguars and Porches. All of this never really appealed to me. I like to keep my life as simple as possible. We live debt-free and I feel that Debbie and I will always have enough money to enjoy life.

Relationship building is a priority for me. I am a thoughtful person, but my impatience with others can overshadow my thoughtfulness. I am sometimes rigid in my thinking, and I can be overly judgmental of others.

At Christmastime, I like to think that I become more humane. I focus more on the good in others, while having higher expectations of myself. I let it be more about me.

With respect to relationship building, I endeavor to bring the good of Christmas into the New Year. In time, through my actions, maybe others will begin to see me as the "Christmas

Guy." I have a long way to go, but this is something for me to work toward.

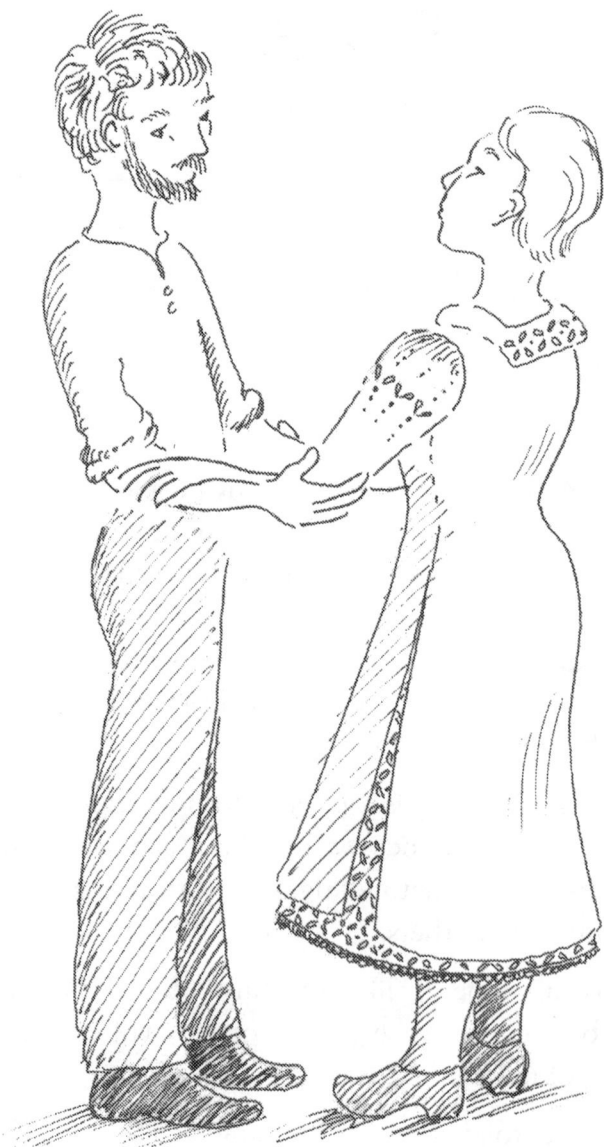

James Hrdlicka

My Best Christmas

"My Best Christmas was my last Christmas.
How could this be with All the rest?"

My Best Christmas was my last Christmas.
A time of Family and Home.
A time to be with Friends that matter.
A time to forgive—and to be forgiven.

There was no snow but I dreamed of snow.
A birthday celebration of Jesus.
Fun and Family and Friends.
I gave it All my best.

My Best Christmas was my last Christmas.
How could this be with All the rest?
I let this Christmas Be, All about Me.
My Best Christmas was my last Christmas.

7. Loved Ones

Christmas is a happy time, but with it comes some tears and heartache. Christmas brings back memories of loved ones that have passed; the ones that are so much a part of our Christmas. The ones that have helped to make Christmas so special for so many years.

I've worked for Mrs. Schaefer for the past six years. A year ago on February 2, she lost her cousin Deborah to liver cancer. They were very close and they had always spent Thanksgiving and Christmas together. This past Thanksgiving and Christmas were different for Mrs. Schaefer. She spent the holidays with family and friends, but without Deborah.

Several weeks after Deborah had passed, Mrs. Schaefer told me that she had lost her best friend. This broke my heart. I could feel her pain. I wrote this poem for her and enclosed it in her Christmas card.

James Hrdlicka

Christmas Tears

New Christmas brings New Tears.
Let them fill your eyes.
Let them overflow your heart.
These are New Christmas Tears.
They remind us of what we held so close
And of what we hold so near.

A new music album was released this year on the occasion of Tony Bennett's eightieth birthday. One of the cuts, "Smile," depicts someone with a broken heart. The lyrics are: "Smile, though your heart is aching—you'll find that life is still worthwhile, if you just smile." Christmas does bring tears, but it also helps us through our tears. I know that Mrs. Schaefer's heart ached for her best friend, Deborah, but she smiled all through Christmas. It's the special angels in our lives that make Christmas what it is.

8. Karen and Bob

On this Saturday afternoon, February 24, I await my flight from Manchester, New Hampshire, to Charlotte, North Carolina. My brother-in-law Bob was diagnosed a week ago with cancer in both his lungs and liver—he's terminal. I'm going to say "goodbye" to someone who's always been very good to me. Most important, he was good to my sister Karen before her passing two years ago. They had been married since 1963.

Karen and Bob moved to Rock Hill, South Carolina, from Los Angeles, California, in 1998. Debbie and I visited them back then. We were so happy to be together again on the East Coast. The last time that I saw Karen is when she came to New Hampshire for a weekend visit in 1996. I mixed up some frozen strawberry daiquiris that July weekend. We sat out on the front deck and we laughed and laughed! Karen's "baby brother" had gotten his older sister "looped"! She didn't ever have to tell me that she loved me. I felt it! I knew it!

Debbie and I had flown down to Rock Hill for Karen's funeral just two years ago. Debbie wanted to come this time, too, but it made better sense for her to stay back to keep the woodstove going and to care for Kallee and Anna. Anna is our almost two-year-old cat-kitten. So, I am flying to Rock Hill to see Bob for the last time. He's family!

James Hrdlicka

Family

Family is a gift from God,
As in the sounds of nature,
As in the tear of a warm embrace.

A family is Thanksgiving, then Christmas,
As in the warmth of an old house,
As in the spicy smell of baking pumpkin pie.

A family is always present,
As in a laughing moment,
As in a crying memory.

Hold on tightly—it will never leave you.
The winds will blow and the tides will turn.
Hold on tightly—don't ever let go.

Bob didn't sleep well on the Saturday night that I arrived. He missed church for the first time in years. I had planned to go with him on Sunday morning. Even though he wasn't able to go with me, I got up and drove to his church instead of sleeping late. I found the Episcopal Church of Our Savior in Rock Hill just before 8 a.m.

I felt as though I had gone to church in Bob's place. I prayed that he would be comforted through his illness. I prayed for my sister Karen. I prayed for my sister Jayne and for my niece Jessica —they moved in with Bob after Karen's passing. I prayed for my mother and for my angels. I prayed for me.

As I waited for my flight back to Manchester, I felt good about my visit with Bob. I had spent my time wisely. Most of the time, Bob and I sat at the kitchen table. We talked about the past and the present. It felt good to be with him this one final time.

As he walked me out of his house that Monday afternoon, he thanked me for coming. Afterwards, I thought that it should have been me thanking him. Through the years, he enriched my life in so many ways. He and Karen "opened up the world" a bit to me by treating me to "dinners out" (we never went out to dinner at home) and even taking me shopping for a sports jacket that I needed for a special event. But most of all, it was just their generous and good nature that meant so much to me as a young man.

🌲 🌲 🌲 🌲 🌲

It is such a treat for me to be sitting here at home writing on this bright and sunny March 4 Sunday morning. For the past two days, I've been cleaning up after Friday's eight-inch mix of snow and drizzle. No more shoveling, roof raking and snow blowing until March's next New Hampshire snowfall!

As I look outside at winter's beauty, the sun is feeling warmer, the days are getting longer, and Daylight Saving Time is scheduled for next Sunday morning. Winter arrived this year a month or so late. It truly looks like early February out there. I joke to Debbie that we'll get snow in July this year. Maybe I'd better stop joking so much.

9. The Smiths

In June 1968, my family and I moved from Queens to Upstate New York. We moved to a rural place called Highland Mills, New York. My mom loved us dearly, and she loved my father. Unfortunately, my mother lacked the courage to free herself and her children from our alcoholic and abusive father. June of 1968 proved to be a turning point in my life. I met the Smiths!

At that time, I met Greg in his backyard shooting baskets with his cousin, Frank. Greg was born in Brooklyn before his family moved to Highland Mills. He was intrigued when I told him that I had just moved from Queens. We instantly became friends, and later, brothers. Our birthdays happened to be the same year (1952) and just three months apart—but I was older!

Greg's parents were genuinely pleased to meet me, as were his younger siblings, Kathy, Kevin, and Lynn. Even Baron, their collie/German sheppard mix, looked happy to see me—he must have known at first sight that I was a dog lover.

Except for Sunday afternoons at my grandmother's house, I

was for the first time in my life exposed to a functional family life. Everyone had something to say at the dinner table. There was no silence! At the same time, everyone was listened to. This was so new and appealing to me. I quickly became a regular at the Smith's dinner table.

After graduating high school and beginning community college, I moved in with the Smiths. I referred to the Smiths as "Mr. and Mrs. Smith," but they were, in fact, my angels on earth. The only difference now, almost forty years later, is that they are in heaven. If it hadn't been for my angels, I wouldn't have survived "the popular and inviting" drug culture of the early 1970s.

Mr. and Mrs. Smith took Christmas very seriously. The week prior to Christmas they bought a large Christmas tree so that it could be set up and decorated in the upstairs living room on Christmas Eve. They were quite impressed with my patience in putting the tinsel on strand by strand. They were more accustomed to their daughter Kathy's "apply-in-clumps-using-a-hair-dryer" method.

On Christmas Eve, after returning from midnight mass, Mr. Smith became Santa Claus with Mrs. Smith right there at his side. All the gifts were hidden at Uncle Moe's office in town or at the Begg's house next door. When the kids awoke at daybreak, the entire space under the tree was packed with presents. Each of them had their designated "overflow areas" in the room for all the presents that wouldn't fit under the tree. My space became the far side of the couch, next to Greg's spot.

I can still vividly see the twinkle in Mr. Smith's eyes on Christmas morning as he captured the joy in the room with his Polaroid movie camera as everyone opened their gifts with vigor. Mrs. Smith, with coffee mug and buttered toast close at hand, enjoyed the scene from the crowded sofa. On Christmas morning, Mr. Smith once again took on the role of Santa Claus!

Santa Claus

Where is the spirit of Santa Claus?
The North Pole; how far is that?
Kindness, wonder, warmth, joy,
Love, peace, tenderness.

This spirit, It's within, and all around,
In our thoughts,
Our words,
Our deeds.

It's in a vision of hope; a dream.
It's a reaching out; a gift from the heart.
It's a kind word; a smile; a gesture.
It's in the silence of a winter's night.

It's in the snowy white; in desert sand.
In valleys below; on mountains high.
It's in the shopping malls and in city streets.
It's in beloved memories of special times.

Kindness, wonder, warmth, joy,
Love, peace, tenderness.
It's as near as a snowy sky,
And true as a fire's warmth.

Look, Listen.
        See, Feel.
        Give, Receive.
Santa Claus is here, now, within, and all around.

🎄 🎄 🎄 🎄 🎄

It's been a week since leaving my brother-in-law Bob in Rock

Hill and landing back home in Manchester. I'm afraid of heights and I'm claustrophobic. Walking down the center aisle of that small jet plane with my head just inches from the ceiling reminded me of being on a Greyhound bus with wings. The bus stays on the ground; the jet plane doesn't.

I am so very happy to have my feet on the ground. I am appreciating being home again in my familiar surroundings. The air smells sweeter and food tastes better. I am grateful to hear familiar voices and to see familiar faces in my town of Hancock. This is Christmas in March!

10. The Night before Christmas

When I was a child, the night before Christmas was magical. Before bedtime we left hot cocoa mix and a plate of cookies on our kitchen table for Santa. And, of course, some carrots for his reindeer. As we slept this night, Santa would make his way down the artificial fireplace in our living room and do his magic.

On Christmas morning, my sisters and I tip-toed into the dining room to the sight of beautifully wrapped gifts under the Christmas tree. Upon entering the kitchen, an empty cup of cocoa lay on the kitchen table surrounded by cookie crumbs.

At bedtime, my mom covered me. I was so excited. I thought about Santa coming. I wanted it to be morning! I knew that I must go to sleep so that Santa could come. I hoped for Christmas morning. I hoped to sleep quickly.

After moving in with the Smiths, I remember coming home late at night on many occasions. Mrs. Smith would be half asleep in her Laz-E-Boy chair as I walked across the living room floor. I dreaded the thought of having to get up early for school or work that morning. During these times of distress, Mrs. Smith, with her sense of humor, would affectionately tell me to "sleep fast." This expression of hers must have inspired me to write "Wake Me Up to Christmas" years later.

Wake Me Up to Christmas

This night is quiet; this night is still.
Let me sleep quickly.

Wake me up to the sights and sounds
Of Christmas morn.
And wake me to the Joy—and Love
And Peace—of Christmas.
Wake me early—to your Presence
And to All that is here.

This night is quiet; this night is still.
Let me sleep quickly.

11. Dear Sister

As children, we were not allowed to use the telephone. My father felt that the telephone was for adult use only. Today, I rarely use the telephone for social purposes. I feel somewhat uncomfortable while speaking on the phone. However, at Christmastime it's different for me. I have a need to be in contact with loved ones. I want and need to "BE in Christmas."

Two weeks before Christmas last, I telephoned my sister Jan. She lives northwest of Los Angeles in Sunland, California. I was thinking of her and telephoned for the sake of saying hi.

Jan is as close to being my twin as I could imagine. I'm her older brother by nineteen months. We live on opposite corners of the country, but I always feel close to Jan. We spent our childhood together. I especially miss her at Christmas.

She shocked me when she asked me why I didn't love her as a child. I couldn't imagine why such an idea occurred to her. How could she have felt this way?

Growing up in Queens, New York, older brothers didn't "hang out" with their younger sisters. That would have made me a sissy. Unconsciously, I had distanced myself from her without knowing the hurt that I had caused. I felt ashamed of myself.

I can't go back. If only I could go back for Jan's sake. If only I could go back for my sake. I asked her forgiveness on that Friday afternoon, December 12. She forgave me.

Jan helped to make my last Christmas my best Christmas. She sent Debbie and me a package containing her homemade cookies and chocolates. The package weighed at least five pounds! I had to freeze some of the peppermint bark, peanut butter bark, and rocky road bark. From time to time, I take a small portion from the freezer to enjoy. As I treat myself, I can taste and feel the many shades of Jan's Christmas colors.

Christmas Colors

Decorate a tree and
Fill a church with flowers.

Wrap a gift and
Hang a wreath up on the door.

Deck the hall with
Boughs of holly and…

What colors will you wear?

White for your childhood innocence and sincerity?
Green for your caring and compassion?
Red for your sense of humor and laughter?
Blue for your truth and honesty?
Pink for your kindness and love?

See as snow coats the ground.
Breathe the fragrance of Christmas.
Hear Santa Claus.
Feel the good of past and now,
Touch the spirit of others.

Look up to the light and
Wear your true colors.
BE a rainbow of Christmas colors.

12. Sweetest Angel

A miracle happened for us in the spring of 1996. Debbie was pregnant! After years of trying to have a baby, a miracle happened. Medical tests had indicated that Debbie wouldn't be able to have a baby. After the frustrations of trying to adopt a child and giving up—Debbie was pregnant!

Our joy lasted for only seven weeks before the miscarriage, but it was seven weeks that I will always cherish. The due date was to be December 24, Christmas Eve. We "knew" that it would be a girl and that she would be "Christina Marie." Marie was Mrs. Smith's first name.

After almost eighteen years of marriage, we would be able to celebrate Mother's Day in our home. That Saturday afternoon, the eve of Mother's Day, I went out to buy Debbie some flowers. That Saturday night, our miracle came to an end.

Debbie had accepted the fact that she would not be a mother years before her pregnancy. To accept it once again must have taken all of the great depth of her inner strength and resilience.

She went back to school to earn a master's degree in psychology. This was enough to fill her void of not being able to have children. Today she counsels children and she loves her work.

For me the void exists, but it is softened by the realization that I am happy in all other facets of my life. I worked for years at Crotched Mountain Rehabilitation Center in Greenfield, New Hampshire. The cure for feeling sorry for one's self is to walk through the brain injury ward of a rehabilitation center. As long as I have my good health, I have it all. I do have it all!

This last Christmas Eve, I lay in bed next to Debbie as morning's first light appeared. I felt the strong presence of our Christina Marie. I got up out of bed, brewed a pot of coffee, and wrote to Christina Marie.

Christina Marie...
We'll Always Be Right Here for You

You woke me from my sleep this early morn,
Mom didn't feel me cry,
To let me know You're here
On this, your Special Day.

You would have been just ten today,
On this Special Christmas Eve Day.
I would have helped you with your homework.
I would have helped you tie your shoes.

You'll need to wait for Mom and Me.
Our greatest Joy will be to meet our Sweetest
Angel.
We'll Always Be right Here for You,
On this, Your Special Day.

13. Merry Christmas!

Have you noticed that in recent years that there's been a shift from "Merry Christmas" to "Happy Holidays"? Christmas cards are commonly referred to as "holiday" cards and Christmas shopping catalogs, of which you've probably received no less than a hundred in December, are now "holiday" catalogs.

After Christmas, two of our nephews sent their Aunt Debbie and Uncle Jimmy thank-you notes and a "happy holiday" greeting! I know that in America today there are many traditions to be honored at this time of year. But I do miss hearing and seeing "Merry Christmas!" Instead, the all-inclusive "Happy Holidays" pervades. What happened to Christmas?

The Hancock fire station is just a mile down the road from our house. There's a bulletin board outside the fire station. Currently the printed message reads, "Keep Warm Safely." During the weeks prior to Christmas of 2005 and again in 2006, the message "HAPPY HOLIDAYS" appeared. The Christmas prior to that, "SEASONS GREETINGS!" was posted. What about Christmas?

Again I submitted a letter to the *Monadnock Ledger*, just in time for CHRISTMAS! It read:

THEY RAN OUT OF LETTERS?

Maybe I was up too late last night wrapping Christmas presents, but a funny thought occurred to me while reading "HAPPY HOLIDAYS" on the fire station message board this morning. Maybe it has to do with the fact that my wife always tries to find the good in every situation, no matter what! She is always quick to justify the questionable actions of others, no matter how unlikely her explanation.

The amusing thought I had was that maybe they just ran out of the letters that spell, "Merry Christmas." Maybe they just ran out of the letters that spell, "Happy Chanukah!" Maybe they only had enough letters to spell out the generic message, "Happy Holidays!"

On a more serious note, we better not allow ourselves to "run out of the letters" that spell out the rich tradition and spiritualism that has always been the substance of who we are as a people. Without our roots and rich traditions, we will become a lost people!

Feel free to wish your neighbors a "Merry Christmas" or a "Happy Chanukah." It feels good to do so at this very special time of the year.

Two years ago at Christmas Eve mass, Father Gerry of Divine Mercy Church made it very clear to his congregation that Christmas remains special. In his sermon, he stated with conviction that, "Christmas is not a holiday; Christmas is a Holy Day."

Good for you, Father Gerry!

14. The Big Picture

Each New Year's Eve, I jokingly say to Debbie, "I wonder if I made my million this year?" As I woke up on Sunday morning, December 31, 2006, my first thought was not of money—it was about the beauty of winter in our front yard. It had snowed a little more than an inch overnight! Up to this point in the season, we had had only a dusting of snow in early December. The ground was white and beautiful again.

After lighting the woodstove and brewing a percolator of coffee, Kallee and I started outside to the truck. We had to drive down to School Street to clean up the one inch of snow that had fallen on the paths that lead to Genie's birdfeeders. Genie takes very good care of the birds that reside in her yard.

On the drive home, Kallee and I stopped at the field behind the firehouse. It glistened in that beautiful morning snow. As I walked around the field with Kallee on that beautiful winter morning, I laughed at the thought of making a million dollars. It just didn't matter!

Did I Make My Million This Year?

Did I make my million this year?
Should I dare to check my book?
Up early this last morning, to light a cold wood
stove.
Then up, and out, to sweep the sunny snow.

A walk around a snowy field,
The morning cold feels good.
A woolen scarf wrapped tightly 'round my neck,

Kallee runs to catch a ball.

James Hrdlicka

Back home to fill my coffee cup,
And then I seed "my" birds.
The church bell rings nine times from town,
In the cold crisp morning air.

It was happy and healthy and wonderful.
This year was not so wealthy again,
But it was oh so Rich.

As we evaluate our lives each year, money is certainly a factor. We all need money to pay our bills and to buy food and services. However, looking at the big picture, money is very much overrated. If we have good health, meaningful relationships, and work that fulfills us, we quite simply have it all. I have it all!

15. Bringing Out the Best

Christmas brings out the best in most people. It's a time of giving, receiving, and sharing with others. It's a time of reflection. Christmas happens at just the right time of the year, right before the New Year begins.

What a nice way to begin a new year, with the Christmas experience close at hand. I like to think that I can make Christmas last well into the New Year. I never want the magic of Christmas to end.

The New Year is an opportunity for a fresh start. It's a time to establish new goals for ourselves. It's a time to "get it right." The New Year is a mystery about to unfold. What will this New Year bring? We enter in hopeful anticipation.

January's Door

Enter with a smile—or with a frown.
Enter boldly through, or on quiet tip-toes.
It will swing freely open or squeak ajar in hesitation.
With or without you,
It will open, fully in time,
But with no guar-an-tees!

Your room will have new candlelight,
Or another shade of gray.
You'll be more wise and new,
Or just more blue and gray.
Enter, enter-in-your-own-way.
There are no guar-an-tees!

Approach with love and respect for others.
Move in with kindness and passion for life.
February's door is just a vision,
January's next—a dream.
Move forward, move ahead.
There are no guar-an-tees!

With love, respect, kindness, and passion for life—
Approach, move in.
With love and respect,
Approach, move in.
With kindness and passion for life,
Approach, move in.

Approach, move in.
Approach, move in.
Approach, move in—through January's Door.
Happy New Year.

James Hrdlicka

16. Uncle Harry

Have you ever known anyone with the gift of making others feel special? People with this gift make us feel good about ourselves. They take an interest in us. They make us "light up" like Christmas trees when we're in their presence! They help us to laugh. If you've been fortunate in knowing someone with this gift, that person will immediately come to mind.

My Uncle Harry had this gift. He was my brother Greg's uncle, but Uncle Harry was "everybody's" uncle. He made me feel like I was the only other person on the planet when we spoke. He was interested in me and he gave me fatherly advice. I miss Uncle Harry for his genuineness, candor, and his loving sense of humor. Additionally, he was quite the jokester. Greg "forgot" to mention this before my first encounter with him!

Upon meeting Uncle Harry in 1968, he turned his shoulder and elbow up toward the ceiling and looked directly into my eyes as he was about to shake my hand. I was a shy kid back then, and I didn't know exactly how to respond at the time. I awkwardly twisted me arm and hand upward to reach his. I found myself bobbing up and down with each shake of his hand. I politely turned beet red as he asked, "How long you been sick, son?"

When I think of people with Uncle Harry's special presence, I wonder how they might have acquired their gift. Were they born with it or did they learn it from something or someone? I wonder, can I learn it?

As April's door is about to creak open, I want and need to bring Christmas forward into a new month. Thoughts of Uncle Harry and his fun-loving spirit will surely bring a smile to my face. And I feel that he'll be watching as I enter through April's door.

The wonder of Christmas began over two thousand years ago in a manger in Bethlehem. Our Savior Jesus was born. As wonderful as this event was, I experience the true wonder and magic in what I bring to Christmas today, in Christmas "present."

The writing of this book began on January 2. Writing it has helped me to take the magic of Christmas into the third week of March. That's a new record for me! I have been a better person through my actions. I wake up most days thinking about how I can make the present day more like Christmas Day. The writing of *Christmas Present* has been just that, a Christmas present.

17. In God's Hands

It's March, and I'm looking outside at winter's beauty. . . . That's right, it snowed another twelve inches on the eve of St. Patrick's Day. Again, it truly looks like early February out there.

I will remember St. Patrick's Day 2007 as the Saturday that I got up at 6:15 a.m., got out at 8 a.m. to snow blow our 500-foot driveway and start a path from the carport to our front steps. As I left our house at 9:15 a.m. to begin a full day of shoveling and snow blowing for my customers, Debbie kissed me goodbye and then headed back to "my" rocking chair next to an inviting woodstove. Kallee watched as I left, but she was also happy to stay home and have a day off with Debbie.

Upon returning home at 6:30 p.m., I stood in front of the woodstove so as to melt the caked-on ice that had crusted over my bootlaces over the past ten and a half hours. So good to get those boots off! So good to be right here in my home on this beautiful day after St. Patrick's Day, Sunday morning. Once again, it's "Christmas in March!"

My sister Jayne called to tell me that Bob is confined to a hospital bed; he can no longer walk. He is, I suppose, waiting and wanting to die. The "hopeful" news is that he is in no pain as the cancer takes his life and that he's in God's hands now. "God bless you, Robert. I'll miss you."

🎄 🎄 🎄 🎄 🎄

Bob was able to leave the nursing home on April 7. He was able to leave all of the pain and frustration that his illness had caused. He returned "home" to my sister and to his angels in heaven.

🎄 🎄 🎄 🎄 🎄

If you're ever in the southwest corner of New Hampshire in the town of Hancock, I'm easy to find. I'm the guy that drives the red Toyota truck with the red Christmas bow. I will be mowing a lawn or blowing leaves from it. I will be shoveling snow or raking snow from a roof. Kallee will be tied to a tree in the woods or running freely as she comes to meet you. She is a very social being; she loves everybody!

If Kallee could speak, she would tell you that she's very well cared for. She would tell you that her coat is brushed every day and that she's well fed. She would tell you that she enjoys her occasional visits to the local nursing home.

Back at our house, she would say: "I don't like the sound of the blowing wind. Jimmy sleeps next to me, on the floor, on very windy nights. Jimmy, he takes me for rides in the truck and lets me run like the wind whenever it's safe to do so. Jimmy always has a pocketful of treats; I earn them for coming when he calls and for bringing the ball back to him and for 'sitting' and 'staying' and for just 'being good'. He kisses me on the top of my head a lot! And, oh, er . . . he's right over there. That's my 'dad'; that's the Christmas Guy."

Author's Note

The writing of this book provided me the opportunity to go back over all of my Christmas writings since Christmas 1991. In doing so, it took me back to Christmas Past. Tears flowed steadily as I revisited all of my Christmas angels. This, indeed, was an extra Christmas present for me.

I write at Christmas because it helps me to "Be in Christmas." Writing helps me to acknowledge my Christmas-inspired thoughts. Writing helps me to better "live" and "feel" Christmas.

I rely on the spirit of Christmas to motivate me to be something better than my usual self. Christmas is special, and I need to be a "more special person" because of Christmas. This is the one time of the year when I'm content and motivated to "cut others a little bit of slack." Inconsiderate drivers and self-absorbed people have little effect on me at Christmastime.

I write approximately fifty Christmas cards and envelopes with red and green calligraphy pens. I include that year's poem with Christmas cards for family and close friends. My sister, Lynn, must like my poems. She displays them at the entryway to her kitchen. I see them there when we travel to her home for the annual "May party."

Most family members rarely make mention of my poems, but that's all right. I like to think that they look forward to reading them. No one's ever asked me to stop writing them. I suppose that's a good sign. Truthfully, I write them mostly for me. Like I said, I need and want to "Be in Christmas."

List of Poems

About the Author

James A. Hrdlicka lives in the scenic Monadnock Region of southwestern New Hampshire. He lives with his wife of twenty-nine years, Debbie, their black Lab, Kallee, and a cat named Anna May.

He is a 1976 graduate of The State University of New York at Plattsburgh. He earned his bachelor's degree in mathematics education with an additional thirty graduate credits in education.

He has worked in education and in human services for twenty-two years. For the past seven years he has been self-employed, performing landscaping, housekeeping, and pet sitting services.

James enjoys taking long walks along the back roads and trails of New Hampshire with his wife, Debbie, and their dog, Kallee. Together they have logged many miles along the beautiful beaches of New Hampshire and southern Maine.

What do I want most for Christmas this year?

What can I do this Christmas to make it more special than last Christmas?

My Favorite Christmas Memories

People that have made my Christmases special through the years

What will I do to bring Christmas Magic into the new year?